CONTENTS

Introduction

Dedication

To my house bunny, Carolina

INTRODUCTION

The Really Useful Bunny Guide is based on my experience in looking after rabbits, my own companion bunny and those who have stayed at my 'Bunny Hotel'.

From the very beginning I wanted my book to be full of practical ideas and advice, as well as insights into rabbit psychology, behaviour and training. This is why I've devoted many pages to body language and the sounds rabbits make, 'bunnyproofing' your home and finding ways to keep your pet busy and content.

This is the book I would have wanted when I first bought my rabbit and I had so many questions about my new pet. I hope it prepares you for day-to-day life with your bunny and that it appeals to both new and experienced bunny owners.

Many thanks to Meg Brown, Carina Norris of *Wild About Animals* and Linda Dykes of the British Houserabbit Association. I would also like to thank my bunny, Carolina, who was often found dozing under my desk while I was writing this book, and all the other bunnies I have looked after.

Carolina James

1 UNDERSTANDING RABBITS

Life in the wild

Wild rabbits live in colonies consisting of 8–15 members; each group has a well-defined social structure with male rabbits fighting to establish and defend their position and both a male and a female leader. Rabbits live in complex underground warrens, made up of several 'rooms' (burrows) linked by narrow exit tunnels. Female rabbits dig the warren using their front paws to loosen the soil and their strong back legs to kick it away and this is where they retreat to raise their young. Rabbits are *crepuscular*: they sleep in their burrows during the day and usually emerge to feed at dawn and dusk when their enemies are not around. Warrens are kept clean and tidy – wild rabbits use the same spots each time they relieve themselves. A pet rabbit also:

- dozes off for several hours during the daytime and then feels active and energetic in mornings and evenings;
- tends to do its business in just one or two places – a habit which can be used to our advantage when litter-training;
- feels instinctively at home in a place which resembles a dark burrow or tunnel, such as in its nest-box, under a bed or behind the settee.

Rabbits are often accused of being cowardly and running away from danger, but this is essential for their survival in the wild where they are hunted by many predators and have very few defences. Even then, they do not always back down and avoid confrontation; they can be very brave and sometimes attack and scare away their enemies.

Wild rabbits survive because they

- only emerge from their warrens when it is relatively safe to do so (usually in semi-darkness);
- stay together and warn each other of potential dangers by thumping their back feet;
- never wander too far from their burrows – this would be dangerous because they have not got the stamina to run long distances;
- are alert to danger and always proceed with caution;
- have speckled grey/brown coats for camouflage;
- are very quiet and do not make noises which might draw attention to themselves;
- are extremely agile and can move very quickly;
- are intelligent and adaptable;
- immediately return to their burrow or dive under a bush when danger threatens;
- make lots of babies, just in case.

No matter how tame and domesticated your pet is, its behaviour remains very similar to that of a wild rabbit. If you have decided that a rabbit is the right pet for you it is a good idea to get to know as much as possible about its behaviour and needs. Rabbits are peaceful and good-natured; usually they do not attack unless provoked or misunderstood. They are good with children and the elderly and are also very quiet. In our homes, rabbits learn to make do with very little space, but you have to remember that it is not natural for a rabbit to live in a hutch (often with no other member of its species). Rabbits as pets deserve the best possible living conditions and the chance to move around freely in a safe and stimulating environment. They also need warmth, affection and companionship. If your bunny is lonely or bored, it is up to you to do something about it. In return your pet will respond by becoming friendly and affectionate and a very special family member.

Hearing

A rabbit's ears are very attentive to sounds; they move in all directions like a TV aerial and can turn independently of one another in order to pinpoint the faintest noise (a rabbit's field of hearing is 360°). Rabbits instinctively stop in their tracks when they hear a loud or unfamiliar noise; if they are very worried they may lie flat on the ground or run for cover. It is very important to be considerate and do things quietly when your bunny is around; if your indoor bunny likes to keep you company when you watch television or listen to music, keep the volume reasonably low to avoid frightening your pet.

Smell

A rabbit's sense of smell is very keen and its nose is always twitching in order to pick up the faintest smells. Rabbits mark their territory by rubbing their scent onto things (chinning) and by leaving their droppings and urine in key places. In the wild this is how they signpost the way from their burrow to feeding places and this is how your pet finds its way around the house and garden. Rabbits proceed very cautiously when they smell something unfamiliar (for instance, another rabbit's scent). Having sensitive noses, they dislike the smell of strong household cleaners, cigarette smoke, perfumes and some cooking smells (not all cooking smells annoy rabbits). You should use only mild, non phenol-based detergents when cleaning your rabbit's hutch (check the product ingredients on the label); if in doubt, ask your vet for advice.

Eyesight

Rabbits have large eyes placed on the sides of the head, which give them a wide panoramic view with a field of vision of approximately 360°. Their close-up sight is fairly limited – this is why your bunny tends to run between your feet and often seems unable to distinguish nearby objects. Rabbits can see better long distance (in the wild they need to be able to spot their enemies in good time) and in dim light. Because their eyes show poor adaptation to light changes, rabbits cannot see well in bright sunlight (suddenly turning the lights on will dazzle your rabbit as well).

Taste

Rabbits can be very fussy about their food. They enjoy eating a variety of things and each rabbit develops its individual preferences. However, rabbits' taste buds have only a limited capacity to recognise harmful substances and, contrary to what many people think, rabbits do not always know what is good for them (see my list of poisonous plants on pages 20–21) or when to stop (for instance, rabbits find herbs irresistible but these should be fed only in moderation).

Touch

Rabbits use their delicate whiskers to find their way in the dark and, in the wild, to measure the width of burrows – rabbits' whiskers are as long as the body is wide. Whiskers are very important to your bunny and they should never be pulled out, cut or touched unnecessarily. The whole of a rabbit's body is very sensitive to the touch so, if your rabbit is worried about something, stroking and petting will have an instant soothing effect.

Rabbit noises

As you spend time with your pet, soon you will realise that rabbits are far from silent and know how to make themselves understood. Here is a short guide to rabbit noises and what they mean.

Soft grinding of the teeth Not all rabbits do this, but it means your bunny is happy. You will probably hear this sound when you stroke your pet in its favourite spots, such as behind the ears or on the cheeks and forehead. Do not confuse this with loud grinding of the teeth, which means your bunny is in pain and should be taken to see a vet immediately.

Soft cooing My bunny does this when she is playing or when I am about to give her a favourite treat, so I take this to be a sign of well-being.

Muttering Rabbits often make short scolding sounds if they are unhappy or angry about something. My rabbit always mutters when I stop petting her, as a way of expressing her disappointment and demanding more cuddles!

Low-pitched squeaking Rabbits squeak softly when they take their soft pellets from their bottom.

Loud thumping with the back feet Rabbits thump their feet when they are frightened, and in the wild this is their way of warning each other of imminent dangers. Bossy rabbits do it as a threatening gesture if they are angry, or simply to get noticed.

Hissing/growling A short growl or hiss is always an aggressive sound and usually precedes an attack. A rabbit may hiss when it feels threatened or cornered, for example, if you are chasing your bunny and are about to put it in its hutch against its will. If this happens, leave it alone for a while or it might react by scratching and biting to defend itself.

Loud squealing This means your bunny is in extreme pain or in terrible danger. Always keep an eye on your rabbit, since it takes only seconds for something to happen. Very recently, my bunny was grazing peacefully in the garden when a magpie swooped down and repeatedly tried to attack her. Rabbits are vulnerable and defenceless in many situations and, as domestic rabbits do not have a burrow to run to, it is up to us to provide shelter and a safe environment. Rabbits have a sensitive disposition and have been known to die from heart attacks when extremely frightened.

2 KNOWING ABOUT RABBITS

Before you get your first rabbit, it is a good idea to find out as much as possible about what owning one involves. For instance, you could speak to a friend who already owns a bunny, or ask your vet for advice. A good rabbit care manual will also help you to find out whether a rabbit is the right pet for you.

You can buy your rabbit from a good pet shop, directly from a breeder, or an animal shelter may have all kinds of rabbits in need of a home. Your bunny should be:

- at least eight weeks old – younger bunnies still need to be with their mother;
- lively and active, unless it happens to be taking a rest;
- friendly, and interested in what is going on around it;
- healthy. Ask to hold your rabbit and look out for possible problems: runny nose, overgrown teeth, dirty ears, a discharge from the eyes and matted or stained fur, particularly under the tail.

When a rabbit is very young, it can be hard to tell whether it is male or female; even pet shop keepers have been known to make mistakes. To be on the safe side, ask your vet to take a look at your bunny so you are sure it is the sex you want. This is particularly important if you are getting more than one rabbit.

Rabbits come in all shapes and sizes and some require more care than others (Angora and Cashmere, for example), so it is a good idea to shop around and do some research before you buy. A larger rabbit can be more difficult to handle and pick up, particularly for small children, and will also require a much bigger cage than, say, a dwarf variety.

What you need to know

A rabbit is relatively inexpensive to feed, but it needs a comfortable hutch and a large enclosure or run, and these are not cheap. The hutch must be cleaned daily and scrubbed out weekly or it will start to smell and your rabbit will become ill. Rabbits are by nature very clean animals; they do not smell and make ideal indoor pets. They appreciate neat surroundings and soon you will find that your bunny takes a personal interest in the hutch cleaning sessions, as if to make sure the job is done properly.

Rabbits like to keep busy. They are lively and inquisitive and they enjoy doing different things. If your bunny looks bored you must make the effort to keep it happy and interested (see pages 17–18 for some ideas).

Rabbits need a lot of exercise, at least three full hours a day. When you own a bunny you have a sensitive animal in captivity. Rabbits are gentle and patient and generally they are silent, but just because your pet cannot bark or meow to tell you that it is unhappy does not mean that it should be neglected or left in its hutch for hours on end; after all, you would not dream of confining a cat or a dog in the same way. As a responsible pet owner you want to make sure that your bunny stays happy and healthy and has the chance to hop around freely as often as possible.

Rabbits are social animals; in the wild they live in groups. If you can spare the time you can be your bunny's best friend. One rabbit on its own is more like a puppy and becomes very affectionate and dependent on its human family. However, if you are away from home for most of the day you should provide your pet with a companion or it will feel lonely.

Two males (bucks) kept together will fight most of the time. A male and a female are also likely to fight, when they are not busy starting a family! Contrary to what many people think, two females (does) may not always get along once they reach sexual maturity. It is a good idea to get two bunnies right from the start because introducing a second later on is not always successful. Neutering your bunnies (see page 35) increases the chances that they will get on better. If you already own a bunny, the best combination is to get a rabbit of the opposite sex and have both neutered. Introduce the newcomer on neutral territory (eg, the bath tub or a table top); some fighting is normal at the beginning but be prepared to separate the rabbits if necessary. Always place a female bunny in the buck's territory rather than the other way round or she might bite and injure the buck very badly.

A rabbit and a guinea pig sometimes become good friends, but not always and should be kept in separate hutches just in case. Be careful if you have a cat or a dog as they might not want to be friends with your new pet; do not leave your bunny alone with them until you are sure that it will not get hurt. Remember to give lots of attention to all your pets to avoid jealousy. Also, always allow your bunny to familiarise itself with its new home before introducing it to other animals.

11

If you are buying a pet rabbit for your children, remember that they may get bored with it after a while, and then it will be up to you to provide your bunny with the care and attention it needs every day for the whole of its life. This involves much more than just feeding and cleaning up after your pet: it means spending time with it and keeping it company, even if you do not always feel so inclined. The lifespan of the average rabbit is seven to ten years.

A baby rabbit quickly becomes friendly and affectionate. However, it needs to be able to trust you and to feel totally comfortable and secure in your hands. You should always handle your pet bunny gently and never tease it, run after it or hold it against its will. Very young children find this difficult to understand fully so I do not recommend giving a pet rabbit to a child under the age of six.

Both male and female bunnies should be neutered. Every 12 months you need to have your rabbit vaccinated against myxomatosis and Viral Haemorrhagic Disease (VHD) (see pages 40–41).

Finally, unless you can take your bunny on holiday with you, it is important to find someone to look after it while you are away. Ideally, this person should know about rabbits and be willing to let your bunny exercise at least two or three times a day. Occasionally, you can leave your bunny for one or two days, provided you give it clean housing and plenty of food and fresh water.

3 BUNNY'S NEW HOME

You can collect your new pet from the breeder or pet shop in a carrying case or a strong cardboard box with ventilation holes, well padded with hay and straw. Remember that this is stressful for the rabbit, and that it will be much happier if you take it straight home so it can settle as quickly as possible. It is important that you have everything your bunny needs before you take it home, and this includes:

- newspapers and straw to line the hutch floor;
- a heavy food bowl that your rabbit cannot chew or tip over easily;
- rabbit food mix;
- a water bottle;
- a mineral/vitamin stone which your rabbit can gnaw at to keep its teeth in trim;
- toys and a piece of untreated wood;
- hay and a hay rack, so that the hay will not get trampled on and will stay clean;
- a litter tray with litter; and, most important of all,
- a large, comfortable hutch (this can never be too big). If you are getting a baby rabbit bear in mind how large it could grow. Also the hutch should be tall enough to allow your bunny to stand on its back legs. The minimum size for the hutch should be:

90cm x 60cm x 45cm high (3ft x 2ft x 18in high) for a small bunny;
120cm x 60cm x 60cm high (4ft x 2ft x 2ft high) for a medium-size bunny;
150cm x 60cm x 60cm high (5ft x 2ft x 2ft high) for a large bunny;
180cm x 75cm x 75cm high (6ft x 2.6ft x 2.6ft high) for a giant variety.

Unfortunately it is difficult to find large, well-made hutches for sale in pet shops, so I suggest you make your own or ask a carpenter to build one for you.

As soon as you get home, put your rabbit in its hutch and leave it alone for a while. Rabbits are naturally timid and your pet will find all the unfamiliar scents and voices overwhelming on its first day. However, given the opportunity, your rabbit will soon be busy making itself at home, sniffing everything new and generally leaving its scent around the hutch. Your bunny will need a little time to get used to its new surroundings and will start eating, drinking and grooming itself only when it feels comfortable and relaxed, so welcome this as a positive sign. Give it plenty of food and hay and hook the water bottle and mineral lick onto the hutch door. Go and talk to your rabbit soothingly from time to time, using its name often so that it gets used to it quickly.

If your bunny's hutch is to be kept outside, make sure:
- it is in a sheltered position away from strong sunlight and winds;
- it does not rest directly on the ground;
- it has a sloping, overhanging roof to keep your rabbit dry when it rains;
- the hutch doors can be securely locked to prevent cats and other animals getting in;
- your rabbit is kept warm by lining the hutch floor with newspaper and lots of straw.
 If you are keeping the hutch indoors, make sure it is:
- in a quiet corner. Your bunny will become anxious if people keep walking or running past its home and noisy pets such as dogs or birds may disturb it. A rabbit's ears are extremely sensitive so avoid any loud or unnecessary noise which might frighten it, such as slamming doors, children screaming, loud music, and so on.
- in a room where you spend a lot of time so your rabbit does not feel lonely;
- near a window or other source of natural light. However, avoid direct sunlight, particularly during the summer;
- away from bright artificial lights, which can dazzle and annoy your rabbit;
- away from hot radiators or heaters;
- away from draughts, to which rabbits are very sensitive. Always bend down to check that there are no draughts at floor level, for instance, coming from under a closed door. Raise the hutch, if necessary.
- away from strong smells, especially cigarette smoke.
Put a litter tray in the back corner of the hutch to make cleaning out easier.

If you have bought a rabbit cage with bars all round and no proper 'bedroom', your rabbit might feel uncomfortable and rather exposed, especially when it is trying to rest. Provide a wooden box with a round opening for hopping in and out and a hinged roof for easy cleaning (a strong cardboard box will do in the beginning). This will make all the difference to your pet, who will be able to go inside its cosy box whenever it wants some peace and quiet. Do not forget to put a litter tray in one of the back corners of the hutch.

On day two, you can let your rabbit out of the hutch for the first time, but you have to prepare for this properly. In the case of an outdoor bunny you can let it hop around either the whole garden or part of it, as long as the designated area has first been made escape-proof. You can do this easily by using rolls of wire netting minimum 1m (3.4ft) high, with bamboo canes as a support. This type of fencing is easy to set up and soon blends in with its surroundings; it also costs more or less the same as a commercial run. If possible, build a proper enclosure with a gate so you can go in and out easily.

If your rabbit is confined to an enclosure or run it is particularly important that this is in a sheltered position away from strong sunlight and wind; under a tree would be ideal. There are various ways in which you can make this area more interesting for your bunny. For instance you can provide:

- a compost heap for your rabbit to dig and roll in;
- a gnawing log from a fruit tree (apple is best) which has not been sprayed with pesticides;
- a bigger log or tree stump for playing and climbing on;
- crates or wooden boxes for your rabbit to hide in or climb onto;
- a pipe to run in and out of – a rabbit loves anything vaguely resembling a tunnel or burrow which makes it feel safe;

- stones, twigs, leaves and pots of plants for added interest. Move these around from time to time so that your rabbit does not get bored, and leave some space between the pots to make little 'alleyways';
- in the enclosure you can also grow carrots, parsley, sunflowers, marigolds and other things your bunny likes. However, avoid those vegetables and herbs which may give your rabbit an upset stomach if eaten in large quantities (see pages 20–21).

A doe will enjoy digging around the garden. This is only natural, but beware of letting your rabbit go too far or she might escape. I let my bunny dig as much as she wants to, but at the end of the day I always fill in the hole if it is too close to the garden fence. If you are worried that your rabbit might burrow its way out of the enclosure or garden, bury the wire fence at least 30cm (1ft) down into the ground.

In my experience, many of the runs on sale in pet shops are far too small and barely allow a rabbit to stretch its legs. You can make your own by stapling wire netting on to a timber frame. It is important to secure the run by pegging it to the ground or strong winds might blow it away, frightening your bunny. Any run must have a covered area as a retreat from danger, strong sun and bad weather. Because it has a roof, a run is ideal if you cannot watch your bunny all the time it is out in the garden but still want to make sure that it stays safe. However, do not leave your bunny in its run unsupervised for long periods of time nor while you are away from home; a run is no substitute for a hutch and you never know what might happen while you are not looking. Finally, move the run to a different spot every two or three days so your bunny always has a fresh grazing patch as well as a new part of the garden to explore.

If you are keeping your rabbit indoors, let it explore one room at a time to start with. If you try to rush things, the bunny will feel intimidated. Move slowly and quietly and give your pet the chance to find its bearings – it will come hopping to you soon enough if you resist the temptation to crowd around it or pick it up.

A very small rabbit will probably try to hide behind pieces of furniture, such as the fridge, cooker or washing machine. Be prepared for this and for the fact that your rabbit might like it so much behind the washing machine that it refuses to come out. This is also potentially dangerous because no bunny can resist the temptation of chewing on an electric wire (or a telephone cable, as I quickly found out), so keep these well out of reach before an accident happens. You can buy plastic tubing and other cable covers from many hardware shops. It is also a good idea to decide in advance whether some rooms are to be no-go areas to your rabbit, at least until it is litter-trained.

Your bunny will soon start to follow you around the house, so be careful not to step on it or drop things on it, especially hot drinks, food and sharp or heavy objects. Open doors slowly, as the rabbit quickly learns to recognise your footsteps and will wait for you behind the door. Never leave your front door open or even ajar (my rabbit has learnt to push and pull doors open) because it takes only a few seconds for your bunny to escape.

Rabbits quickly learn to hop up and down a few steps and soon go confidently down a full flight of stairs. If your rabbit is not allowed upstairs or downstairs you can use a baby gate or make your own by stapling wire mesh onto a wooden frame. I use a similar gate to stop my rabbit from hopping into the garden if I do not have time to supervise her.

To make your home, or one particular room, more interesting for your rabbit, try one or all of the following:

•Get some strong supermarket boxes of various shapes and sizes and cut doors and windows in them for your bunny to hop in and out. This costs nothing and your rabbit will not get bored if you move the boxes around and replace old boxes with new ones from time to time. Alternatively, you could make one or two wooden boxes (longer lasting and much nicer to look at than supermarket boxes). Ask your local timberyard to cut the wood to the right size, use a jigsaw to cut two or more windows in the side walls, then nail the whole thing together.

•Nail together four lengths of wood about 30 x 90cm (1 x 3ft), to make a 'tunnel' for your rabbit. Your bunny instinctively feels at home in a tunnel because its shape is similar to that of a burrow. It will spend a lot of time hopping in and out of the tunnel or simply hiding in it when it does not want to be disturbed. So far, I have made three of these tunnels and, together with supermarket and wooden boxes, they make an excellent ever-changing playground for my rabbit.

•Leave lots of nooks and crannies behind and between the furniture for your rabbit to hide in and explore. Rabbits particularly like to crawl into dark, out-of-the-way and enclosed spaces.

•Give your bunny one or two chairs, a low, non-slippery table and maybe a sofa and some cushions to hop up and down on. Keep your rabbit away from expensive pieces of furniture; rabbits are no more destructive than other pets but you should always be around during playtimes to make sure that your bunny is safe and does not damage anything.

•Drape a large towel or a dressing gown securely over a chair for your rabbit to play with; this never fails to interest my pet and keeps her busy and contented for ages. When my bunny gets tired she falls asleep under her chair with my dressing gown draped around her like a blanket and only her face and ears sticking out!

•Give your rabbit a straw mat (like the ones you buy for the beach) and any items made of untreated straw, wicker, rattan and so on. Your rabbit will love nibbling at them and, hopefully, will find them more attractive than skirting boards and furniture. You can buy natural straw mats, coasters, bags and even hats very cheaply if you shop around. Placing straw mats or spare bits of carpet in the corners of a room is also a good way of stopping your rabbit from damaging the carpet.

•Leave the travel cage lying around with some hay and straw in it for the rabbit to nibble at. Your pet will soon get used to hopping in and out of it and will stop associating it with unpleasant things, such as being taken to the vet.

•Invest in a comfortable (plastic) dog bed for your bunny to sleep or doze in.

•Buy a large wicker or straw basket (for instance, a moses basket), line it with a bin bag and fill it with hay and straw so your rabbit can dig, munch and do its business at the same time.

•Hide a carrot or green leaf in a basket, plant pot, or under some straw or hay. Your bunny will follow its nose and dig it out when it is hungry.

•Give your bunny a cat or baby rattle (eg, keys) made of untreated wood or hard plastic.

•Buy a football or a ball made of hard plastic for your rabbit to push and roll.

•Many rabbits enjoy tossing the cardboard rolls from inside toilet paper or kitchen paper towels.

•If you have a sheltered balcony or terrace, you could make this into a bunny area, especially during the summer months. Make sure that the floor is not stone cold (cover it with straw mats) and that there are no dangerous gaps in the railings.

4 FEEDING YOUR RABBIT

Rabbits spend a lot of time eating and nibbling and, unlike other pets, need to have food available 24 hours a day. They are very individual when it comes to food – you will soon get to know your pet's likes and dislikes – and they appreciate a varied diet, which is essential to their health and wellbeing. A rabbit's diet consists mainly of rabbit mix, hay and fresh foods.

Rabbit mix

You can supplement this with a piece of Weetabix, half a Krisproll and a piece of wholemeal biscuit every day to add variety and to keep your bunny's teeth in trim. Discard any leftovers after 24 hours and replace with fresh rabbit mix in a clean bowl.

Hay

Hay is best kept in a hay rack to prevent soiling, and should also be replaced daily. Always store hay in a plastic bag with a few holes for ventilation.

Water

Even very young rabbits quickly get used to drinking from a bottle, which is a very convenient and hygienic way of providing water. It is best to buy a bottle with a double-ball valve to avoid constant dripping. Fill your bunny's bottle with fresh water every day and wash it regularly with a spout brush and a narrow bottle brush to prevent algae build-up.

Fresh foods

Rabbits enjoy eating fruit and vegetables, but these should be introduced very gradually into their diet, especially in the case of very young animals. A rabbit cannot be sick if it eats too much of something and, because it has a sensitive tummy, it can easily suffer from digestive problems. Feed between 1–2 handfuls of vegetables and 1–2 tablespoons of fruit daily, depending on the size of your bunny. Wash all fruit and vegetables thoroughly before giving them to your bunny. Only feed fresh fruit and vegetables and never wet or straight from the fridge. Fresh food soon starts to wilt and becomes contaminated with bacteria, so throw it away after 30 minutes if it is left uneaten.

You can feed your rabbit apple, banana, beetroot, broccoli and its leaves, carrot and carrot tops, celery, celeriac, chicory, Chinese leaf, cucumber, endive, fennel, Jerusalem artichoke, kohlrabi and its leaves, melon, parsnip, peas (including the leaves and pods), pear, pumpkin, radish greens, raspberry, strawberry, Swiss chard, green and red tomatoes, watercress, watermelon. In addition you can give (in moderation) herbs such as balm, basil, chervil, coriander, dill, horseradish, lavender, lovage, marjoram, parsley, peppermint, sage, savory. Give your rabbit only small amounts of Brussels sprouts, cabbage, cauliflower, kale, lettuce, maize, mustard greens, potato, spinach, swede and turnip because they may cause digestive and other problems. Avoid tomato leaves, beans, potato sprouts and rhubarb, which are poisonous.

Wild plants

The following wild plants are suitable for your rabbit: avens, agrimony, alfalfa (both fresh and dry), borage, bramble (blackberry), buckwheats, burnet, camomile, caraway, chickweed, white clover, coltsfoot (both fresh and dry), comfrey (let it wilt slightly before feeding it to your bunny), corn marigold, corn spurrey, cowslip, cow parsnip (hogweed), crosswort (maywort), dandelion, dead-nettles, docks (before flowering), fat hen (pigweed or goosefoot), goosegrass (cleavers), goutweed or ground elder (before flowering), groundsel (in moderation because it is a laxative), hawk bit, hawkweed, heather, hedge parsley, knapweed, knotgrass, mallow, mayweed, meadowsweet, mugwort, tender nettle shoots (also dried), nipplewort, orache, oxeye daisy, plantain, sainfoin, shepherd's purse, silverweed, sow thistles (milk thistles), tare (vetch), trefoil, wild carrot and yarrow (both fresh and dried). Avoid red clover, which causes bloating, and the following plants: arum (cuckoopint), bindweed, bluebell, bryony, buttercup (although this is harmless when dried), greater and lesser celandine, colchicum (meadow saffron), corncockle, cowslip, dog's mercury, elder (although it is quite safe before flowering), bigwort, fool's parsley, foxglove, ground ivy, hemlock, henbane, kingcup, milkweed, nightshade (all types), ragwort, scarlet pimpernel, spurge (euphorbia), toadflax, traveller's joy and wood sorrel.

Twigs

Rabbits love nibbling on twigs and those with buds and tender shoots are a particular delicacy. You can collect twigs and branches from many fruit trees and practically all deciduous trees and bushes: apple, birch, blackberry, fir trees, hazel, hawthorn, maple, pear, raspberry, spruce trees and willow. Avoid acacia, apricot, azalea, beech, box, cherry, some clematis species, elder, holly, ivy, laburnum, mistletoe, nux vomica, oak, oleander, peach, periwinkle, plum, privet, rhododendron, rosewood, snowberry, spindleberry, thorn apple, waxplant, wisteria, yew and most evergreen trees and shrubs.

Leaves

Leaves should be collected in the spring when they are as young as possible and have a high nutritional value – older leaves are more difficult to digest. Rabbits like eating the leaves of these trees: acacia (however, the bark of this tree is poisonous so do not feed acacia twigs to your rabbit), apple, beech (young leaves only), birch, blackberry, cherry, grape, hazel, horse chestnut (young leaves only), lime, mountain ash, mulberry, pear, poplar (avoid the leaves of the black poplar, which taste bitter), raspberry and strawberry. Do not feed leaves from peach and plum trees and evergreens because they contain poisonous substances.

Flowers

It is fine for your rabbit to feed on these flowers: aster, carnation, daisy, geranium, geum, helenium, hollyhock, honesty, marguerite, marigold, Michaelmas daisy, nasturtium, rose, stock, sunflower and wallflower. However, avoid acacia, aconite (monkshood), antirrhinum, anemone, brugmansia, columbine, crocus, daffodil, dahlia, delphinium (larkspur), feverfew, gypsophila, hellebore (Christmas rose), hyacinth, iris, lily of the valley, lobelia, love-in-a-mist, lupin, narcissus, poppy, primrose, snowdrop, tulip and other bulbs.

And remember ...

Never collect plants from the roadside (lead pollution), parks (possible contamination from dogs' urine and excreta) or from areas treated with fertilisers, pesticides, weedkillers and other chemicals. Do not expect your bunny to sense which plants are good and which are poisonous: this is something you have to know and watch out for. Never give your rabbit grass cuttings because these wilt and go mouldy very quickly (grass can be grown easily in a container if you do not have a garden).

Supplements

Give your rabbit a salt lick and a vitamin/mineral block to nibble at. You can also buy milk drops and other suitable treats from the pet shop (feed in small amounts).

Obesity

If your rabbit is overweight, probably it will find it difficult to hop around and do things and, more importantly, to clean itself where it matters most. A fat rabbit may also have a shorter life because its heart has to work harder, so make sure that your rabbit keeps busy, gets enough exercise and eats the right foods. If it is still too well-padded, give it a smaller portion of dry food until its weight has gone back to normal.

5 LITTER TRAINING

It is important to have a litter tray ready from the moment your indoor bunny is first let out of the hutch. Use a paper-based litter or newspaper covered with hay or straw (many rabbits like to nibble at something while they go to the toilet). Avoid pine and cedar shavings and scented or clumping cat litters, which may harm your pet. Place a litter tray with a few droppings inside the hutch (see page 14) and another in a corner of the room, or wherever your bunny likes to urinate. Put your rabbit in its litter tray often, especially after it has finished eating, and hopefully it will get the idea. Alternatively, lure your rabbit to the litter tray with a food treat.

If you are new to litter-training, bear in mind the following points:

- Keep your bunny in one room until it learns to use the litter tray.
- There should be a litter tray in each room your pet is allowed in.
- Keep your bunny away from expensive carpets, cushions and sofas if your pet is not very reliable and particularly if an 'accident' is likely to upset you. Some rabbits love to do their business on something soft and there is nothing more tempting than a bed or armchair.
- If you have blocked off a certain area, your bunny is sure to mark as far as it can go by doing its business just outside it, so this could make an ideal litter tray spot.
- Rabbits urinate heavily and at times there seems to be no limit to the number of pees an individual can do (my bunny's record is six in ten minutes). Learning to recognise when your bunny is about to do its business might save you a lot of cleaning-up afterwards (see pages 30 and 31).

- Spayed and neutered rabbits are easier to litter-train and more reliable and gradually stop spraying (see page 35).

When house-training your pet bunny it is important to persevere and be consistent. You have to expect some cleaning-up during the first few weeks – house-training does not happen overnight. My advice is to be alert in the early days and follow your bunny everywhere. When your rabbit pees in the wrong spot scold it firmly and briefly without raising your voice. It is important that you scold your bunny immediately after it has made a mess as it will soon forget it has done anything wrong and your words will just upset and confuse it. It goes without saying that you should never hit your rabbit, however lightly.

Finally, do not forget to reward your bunny with lots of praise whenever it uses the litter tray (a little treat from time to time is also a good incentive). Make your rabbit feel special and at the centre of attention and, with any luck, it will want to repeat the experience.

6 MAKING FRIENDS

Picking up

Your pet rabbit will quickly become tame and affectionate if you handle it often, but it is vital to know how to do this properly.

It is very important that you do not chase your bunny or it will never learn to trust you. Walk up to it and bend down so that you are at its level. Do not pull or pick up your rabbit by the ears. Get hold of the scruff of its neck with one hand, and scoop up your rabbit without hesitating, which it would sense straight away. Immediately place your other hand under its bottom, then hold your rabbit close to your chest.

Your bunny will probably try to wriggle away, pushing against your body with its powerful back legs. Its speed and strength may well surprise you so I suggest you keep your hand on its neck, just in case. Hold your rabbit securely but always gently and talk to it soothingly so that it knows it is not going to get hurt. If your bunny is very scared (or very bossy) it might scratch and bite you or even try to leap over your shoulder.

Alternatively, hold your bunny facing away from you: put one hand under its forelegs and the other under its bottom, then pick it up. In this position it is more difficult for your bunny to get away because it has nothing to push against. If your rabbit becomes restless hold its back legs in your hand to stop it from kicking out and scratching.

Many rabbits do not like to be off the ground and hurt themselves badly trying to get away; my own bunny gets very anxious when she is being carried so I never pick her up unless absolutely necessary. A rabbit is likely to feel particularly nervous as you bend over to set it down, so be especially careful at this stage since a fall could result in serious injuries and even be fatal.

Please do not let anyone handle your bunny unless they know how to do so safely and correctly. Children in particular might find it difficult to cope with a struggling rabbit, especially a large one; explain to them that your pet should never be picked up against its will or held by the legs or tummy when it tries to get away. Make sure you are always on hand to give advice and assist your children, at least until they are old enough to take on full responsibility for their pet.

Just because your bunny does not like to be picked up does not mean it is unfriendly; it still wants to be cuddled and petted (probably a bunny's favourite activities). However, it could be that your pet:
- is frightened of heights (this is very common in rabbits);
- is very independent and likes to stay in control;
- wants to do something else;
- simply does not feel like it (bunnies have good and bad moods, just like humans);
- has been dropped or handled roughly before, in which case it does not want to repeat the experience in a hurry.

Do not be disappointed if your bunny runs away as soon as you try to pick it up. Respect its wishes and take things gradually. Spending time at its level will make your bunny feel comfortable and gives it a chance to get to know you. Rabbits are by nature curious and interested and your bunny will soon come up to you to investigate. Once your pet knows it can trust you it will not feel nervous or afraid when you try to pick it up.

CHAPTER SIX

My tip
When picking up a rabbit for the first time, sit on the floor rather than stand up. If your rabbit begins to struggle, you will be able to let go of it quickly and safely.

Petting
Bunnies are friendly and cuddly and they like physical contact. Petting your rabbit every day will make it feel happy and relaxed, and it will soon find a way to let you know that it wants to be petted, to the point of becoming very insistent about it.

Always stroke your bunny in the direction of the fur and learn to recognise its favourite spots (behind the ears, on the forehead, cheeks, back and tummy) and least favourite spots (the back legs, the tail and under the chin). Some rabbits can be very touchy about their ears, so it is best to leave these alone. Whiskers are also very sensitive so make sure you do not pull or touch them unnecessarily.

Brushing

It is a good idea to brush your rabbit every day, particularly during moulting, to remove the dead fur. Bunnies love having their backs brushed and sit very still as you do so. Normally you should brush the coat only in the direction that the fur is growing, but every now and again brush it in the 'wrong' direction to check that it is healthy and free from parasites, particularly if you see your bunny is scratching itself a bit too vigorously during grooming. Let your bunny see and smell the brush before you start to use it. Your pet will soon adopt it as one of its possessions by 'chinning' it. Do not leave the brush lying around because it will probably get nibbled.

Much as your bunny likes to be petted and brushed you should never disturb or interrupt it when it is eating, grooming or trying to rest.

Hand feeding

Feeding your rabbit a favourite treat from the palm of your hand (not between the fingers) is also a good way of getting it to know and trust you.

7 TRAINING

Not many people know that a rabbit can be trained to understand and obey a variety of commands. Rabbits are bright and alert and respond well to training; unfortunately, they are also very underrated animals. I have noticed that many owners do not bother to call their pet by its proper name, thinking a rabbit is not intelligent enough to recognise it. In fact, a rabbit gets used to its name in a matter of days if you use it regularly and this is the basis for further training. Training your rabbit is relatively easy and your pet will enjoy having something stimulating and interesting to do. Even older rabbits can be successfully trained, so it is never too late to start. A trained bunny is a friendly, well-behaved pet; however, rabbits are by nature lively and inquisitive and will always tend to do certain things, so don't expect too much!

Decide in advance which commands you want to teach (see the list below for some ideas), and then do one at a time. Keep the command short and simple and always say your bunny's name at the end of it (do not use a nickname or a term of endearment or your rabbit will end up thinking that is its name). Be consistent and always use the same wording to avoid confusing your bunny. Say each command clearly more than once to make it more effective and easy to remember, particularly in the early days.

Rabbits are very sensitive animals so do not raise your voice or lose your temper. Do not be unpredictable, either, because your rabbit needs to be able to trust you and rely on you before it can learn anything. Punishing your rabbit will definitely get you nowhere; rewards, on the other hand, are very useful in getting started and are guaranteed to get your rabbit's attention and make you very popular. Gradually replace a reward with praise and lots of cuddles so that your bunny learns to obey a command even when it does not get a piece of biscuit or a favourite treat at the end of it.

You might want to teach your bunny one or more of the following commands.

Come here (come on), X (where X is your rabbit's name)

Rabbits do not like being chased. The chances are that you will a) never catch your bunny and probably you will look silly in front of all the neighbours; b) chase your rabbit once, and then have to chase it every time; c) make your rabbit so frightened that it starts bumping into things such as walls and furniture, injuring itself badly in the process (rabbits cannot see very well close up).

The trick is to get your rabbit to come to you instead, and here's what to do:
- Put your bunny on a harness and a long lead. Give the rabbit a few minutes to get used to it and feel comfortable and let it lead you rather than the other way round.
- Say 'Come here, X' or 'Come on, X' in a warm tone of voice while tugging gently at your bunny's lead. Gradually make the lead shorter to get your bunny to hop towards you. If you haven't got a lead you can achieve the same results with the help of a food reward.
- Slowly walk up to your rabbit with a treat in your hand. Make sure your pet notices it, that is, let your bunny smell the treat.
- Walk back to where you were originally and, if your rabbit has not followed you already, say 'Come here (come on), X'.

CHAPTER SEVEN

•Hopefully your bunny will come hopping to you on the strength of the reward (if it is hungry enough). Probably you will find that after a couple of times all you have to do is rattle the biscuit tin or food container and your rabbit will be at your feet in a matter of seconds.

Up, X

This is useful if you get tired of spending a lot of time on the floor and want your bunny to come to your level, such as on your lap, on the sofa, and so on. Do not say, 'Come here/on, X' or you will confuse your bunny.

Down, X

I taught my bunny this command without using a reward. Whenever I saw her on the settee (where she is not allowed on her own) I would say this command and then push her gently towards the floor to make my meaning clear. It only took my bunny one week to get the message, and now she knows that whenever I leave the settee she must do the same, however reluctantly.

Home, X

To get your rabbit to return to its hutch, simply walk behind it slowly saying, 'Home, X'. If your rabbit feels it has not had its fair share of exercise, it may run up and down for a few minutes, but eventually it will hop in the hutch to stop being harrassed. Immediately give it lots of praise and a treat, to make this a positive experience. Then close the door gently. If the hutch is raised off the ground, you will have to provide steps or a wooden ramp to help your rabbit get in and out.

Pee pee, X

It is possible to train a bunny to go to its litter tray using this command. For instance, my rabbit knows that she is not allowed to hop on the sofa unless she has visited her litter tray first. Sometimes I have to coax her there with an incentive, which definitely helps to speed things up, but most of the time she does the right thing without needing to be reminded or rewarded. When I see that she is about to hop in the tray I repeat this command, so that by now she knows exactly what it means.

Good bunny, X

Say this whenever your bunny has been good or has responded well to a command. Pet your rabbit as well to add to the praise.

No, X

Say this command every time your bunny misbehaves (not just occasionally). Your bunny will soon learn that it is doing something naughty. The average rabbit can be very persistent and is probably only waiting for you to turn your back to return to whatever it was doing. All I can say is, be patient and persevere. If your bunny insists on misbehaving, scoop it up quickly without making a fuss and say 'No, X'. Put the little rascal in its hutch and leave it there for 10–15 minutes, then let it out again. If you find it difficult to catch your rabbit simply spray it with some water. Do this a couple of times and your bunny, who is a smart bunny, will soon learn.

It is important to keep your pet busy and give it new things to do and explore from time to time. Very often, a naughty bunny is only bored and wants attention, and will do anything as long as it helps to pass the time and gets it noticed.

It's OK, X

Rabbits are very alert to sounds and they sense danger, real or otherwise, well before we do. They often become really frightened about something silly, like a neighbour's car pulling up or the telephone ringing. Saying 'It's OK, X' in a soothing voice will help to relax your bunny and you can use this command whenever your pet is anxious or worried (at the vet's or during a thunderstorm, for example).

Danger, X

Say this whenever a danger appears (such as a cat or dog) and reinforce the command by thumping your foot loudly on the ground. Your bunny will instinctively freeze and then probably bolt or come running to you for shelter. Thumping is what rabbits do in the wild to warn each other that something is wrong.

Thumping your foot or hand on the floor will always stop your bunny in its tracks and make it pay attention. This can be very useful in dangerous situations (for instance, if your pet is eating something harmful but refuses to respond to the 'No' command). Thumping should not be (over)used in the wrong circumstances or it will lose its effectiveness and your bunny will be frightened unnecessarily.

Food, X or Treat, X

This will bring your pet running, and is very useful if you want to get its attention fast. Just make sure that you really have a treat handy and that you are not just saying that or your bunny will feel cheated and will never fall for it again.

Do not spoil your bunny by giving it treats all the time; your pet will quickly get used to this and then expect a reward for everything it does. Give small treats only occasionally, when your rabbit has been particularly good – or when everything else fails!

8 BODY LANGUAGE

It is important to observe your bunny and learn to recognise its body language. This way you will know immediately when there is something wrong or when your bunny is not well.

Light nudging with the nose
This is your pet's way of greeting you, for example, first thing in the morning, and also is a request to be petted.

Forceful pushing away of your hand/foot, etc.
This means your bunny wants to be left alone. Some bossy rabbits will even nip you if you do not get out of their way pretty fast, so be warned. Discourage this kind of behaviour by using the 'No' command (see pages 26–27).

Standing on the back legs
Rabbits stand on their back legs to get a better view of their surroundings or to reach tempting bits of food. My bunny also does this to make herself more visible and to catch my attention when she feels neglected. If you see your rabbit standing upright near a door this is usually a sign that it wants to be let in or out.

Chinning
Rabbits leave a scent (odourless to humans) by rubbing their chins onto anything they want to mark as theirs, including their food bowl, plants, pieces of furniture and even your feet. This makes them feel safe both in their usual surroundings and, more importantly, in an unfamiliar place. The probability is that within seconds of you arriving home with a shopping or school bag your bunny will notice it and chin it, as if to say 'I own this'! My bunny chins her possessions regularly to make sure they were not claimed by another bunny while she was not looking. She is very curious and observant and immediately marks anything new around the house or garden.

Grooming
Rabbits keep their coats clean and shiny by grooming themselves very thoroughly several times a day. When my bunny was ill she stopped looking after her fur and only began doing so again when she was getting better.

Licking
A friendly bunny licks your hands and face to say 'Thank you' and 'I love you', particularly while it is being petted. Sometimes you will find that your bunny gets carried away and goes on licking the floor after you have taken your hand away. Rabbits also express their affection toward each other by mutual licking.

Bunny moves its jaws as if chewing
This means your bunny feels content and relaxed.

Bunny rolls on its back with eyes half-closed

Rolling is always a sign that your bunny feels safe and happy. My rabbit does this after being cuddled or after eating something particularly tasty as a way of showing her appreciation for the good things in life.

Brief shaking of the ears

Rabbits sometimes do this is if they have had enough and want to get away (for instance, when they have been petted or brushed for too long).

Tearing newspapers

This means your bunny is bored and wants something to do, so let it out of the hutch for a while (a rabbit should spend at least three or four hours a day hopping around freely). Newspaper ink is harmful, so if your rabbit gets into the habit of swallowing bits of newspaper you should line the hutch floor with something else.

Chewing

Your bunny's front teeth grow all the time and must be kept in trim. Give your rabbit an apple tree branch, a piece of untreated pine and enough hard foods like carrots and celery stalks to gnaw on. It should become less interested in unsuitable items and, with any luck, it will even ignore them. I also let my rabbit chew on untreated straw mats and coasters, and twigs from various plants such as hazel and willow, whenever possible.

If your rabbit is chewing on something it shouldn't, clap your hands twice to get its attention and say 'No' in a firm tone of voice, then immediately offer it something it is allowed to chew (a grass mat, its own piece of untreated skirting board, etc). You could also try spraying your skirting boards with an anti-chew repellent for kittens or puppies (available from pet shops). This contains a bitter but harmless substance which should deter your bunny from further chewing. Finally, if no amount of training or precautions can stop your pet from nibbling at telephone cables, handbags or the garden hosepipe, you have to be one step ahead of your rabbit and keep these things out of reach at all times.

Scratching

Bunnies often scratch and dig into the ground in order to keep their nails worn down. If your bunny has the opportunity to hop on hard surfaces such as patio tiles, and spends enough time out of the hutch, its nails will probably never need trimming. Rabbits that spend most of their lives indoors or confined in a hutch can have very long nails. Please do not cut your bunny's nails unless you know how to do this properly, and only clip a little bit off the tips to avoid damage to the nails' blood vessels and nerves. You need special nail clippers and also some help (rabbits can be very fidgety in these situations). Ask your vet or vet's nurse to do this for you if you are not sure what to do.

Scratching can also be a sign that a) your bunny is about to do its business; and b) it feels lonely and bored, such as when it stretches up your legs and paws at your clothes for attention.

Digging

Female rabbits often dig around the garden, particularly when they are in heat or pregnant, in order to make a burrow. My rabbit can dig for hours at a time, only resting for a few minutes when she gets too tired, and while she is busy digging she cannot be persuaded to do anything else, not even eating (her favourite occupation) or drinking. This happens a couple of times a year, during which my garden looks like a building site but, thankfully, after a few days she seems to lose all interest in digging and things return to normal.

Circling

Circling around your feet can be a sign that your rabbit wants to mate. You will notice that your rabbit becomes restless when it reaches adolescence and this is the time to have your pet neutered or spayed. Because rabbits are territorial animals, they feel threatened when you clean out the hutch and may run around you in circles or even jump on your back to supervise the proceedings. I suggest you always wait until your rabbit is out of the hutch before you clean it or touch its contents (food bowl, litter tray, etc).

You will find that your rabbit goes round and round you in circles when it wants some attention (a truly dizzying experience). My rabbit also circles my feet in anticipation if I am near her food cupboard and she wants something to eat.

Eating droppings

Do not scold your bunny; this is perfectly natural and should not be discouraged. Rabbits need to digest some foods twice and normally take these droppings, which are softer than the others and kidney-shaped, directly from the anus.

Bunny pushes out its bottom and tail

Your bunny is about to pee (see Litter training on page 22).

Bunny ignores you, turns its back on you or starts grooming

This happens when, for example, you have scolded your bunny and it is your pet's way of making you feel silly and powerless. Do not react by raising your voice, just ignore your bunny back for a while.

Bunny looks tense and worried; it stares with eyes wide open and perks up its ears (unless it is a lop)

This means that your bunny has heard a sudden, loud or unfamiliar noise and is frightened. The 'It's OK' command can be very useful in this situation and your bunny will quickly learn what it means. Stroking your pet and talking to it soothingly also has an immediate calming effect.

Bunny lies flat on the ground with its ears folded back

This is a natural reaction to a loud noise or a dangerous situation and is your rabbit's way of 'hiding' and becoming inconspicuous when there is no other shelter.

Bunny squats in a relaxed way with its ears folded back or lies on its side with its legs stretched out and eyes beginning to close

Your bunny is resting or trying to get to sleep and should not be disturbed.

Bunny points its head and ears forward and extends its tail

This means your rabbit is curious and interested in something but cautious at the same time (when meeting another rabbit, for example).

Bunny points its head forward, folds back its ears and extends its tail

Your rabbit is about to attack and may bite. Stay well clear and do not do anything that might upset it, such as chasing it or trying to pick it up.

Racing around at high speed

Bunnies need to let off steam from time to time, particularly after spending a long time in the hutch. You may have seen your pet suddenly zig-zag around the garden, performing the most amazing twists and leaps. If your rabbit races around the house it might jump over low tables or even bump into things. These high-speed sprints are your bunny's way of enjoying its freedom and keeping fit, and are also a sign that it feels comfortable and at home with its surroundings. They are usually followed by a 'flop' because bunnies get tired fairly quickly.

Spraying urine

This is what males do to mark their territory. In the wild it is very common for a dominant buck to spray its doe(s) as well as subordinate males. A pet bunny also tends to spray its surroundings, including its owners. Spraying can usually be prevented if you have your bunny neutered (see page 35).

It is not only male rabbits that spray, though. My female rabbit used to do this while she was growing up. She does not do much spraying now that she is an adult, except when there is a guest rabbit in the house and she feels that her territory has been invaded.

Rabbit nuzzles its head under another rabbit's chin

This is a submissive gesture; by pushing its head under the other rabbit's chin the first rabbit indicates that it is in a subordinate position. This often happens when a rabbit feels insecure (for instance, if it is in another rabbit's territory) as it is a good way of avoiding confrontation with a stronger and more established animal.

Bunny rushes around with straw in its mouth

Your female bunny is making a nest. If your rabbit is not pregnant, she probably thinks she is (false pregnancies are fairly common in rabbits).

My own bunny goes through five or six false pregnancies a year. So far she has built nests under my bed, under the Christmas tree, and at my feet (which I took as a compliment). Once she even made one under my pillow using straw and soft fur from her tummy. The nest was so neat (there were no bits of straw on the bed) that I did not notice it until the following morning!

Bunny is very quiet and hardly moves or eats; it stares straight ahead with a dull look

Your bunny is probably ill and in pain. If it has not gone back to normal within a few hours, gently put it into its carrying case and take it to the vet. Do not delay doing this because your rabbit's health could deteriorate very quickly without proper medical treatment.

9 HEALTH CARE

You need to take good care of your rabbit to make sure that it stays healthy. You should give it the right food, keep its home clean and dry, and let it exercise at least three or four hours a day. Cuddling and grooming your pet are also very important to keep it happy and healthy.

Sometimes your bunny's resistance to diseases is lowered, for instance, when it is very young or old, when it is moulting or when there is a sudden change in temperature. If you spend time with your bunny every day you will quickly notice any changes in its appearance or behaviour. Look out for the following signs:

- Is your rabbit lively and active?
- Does it move around freely without limping?
- Is it eating normally?
- Does it groom frequently and is the fur glossy and clean?
- Are the eyes bright and without discharge?
- Is the nose clean and dry?
- Do the ears react to the slightest sound?
- Is your bunny's bottom clean?
- What are the droppings like?

Grooming your bunny also helps you to spot possible problems. Look for bare patches in the fur, swellings, wounds and signs of parasites. Check that the skin inside the ears is not crusty or smelly. Look under the paws to see if there are any sores and check that the fur is not matted or dirty. Make sure the toenails and teeth are the right length. If you think something is wrong, take your bunny to the vet straight away. Many illnesses and parasites can be treated easily, provided they are diagnosed in the early stages.

Rabbits make two types of droppings, the dry (faecal) pellets, which should be round and firm, and the soft (caecal) pellets, which are shiny and moist and usually grouped together. Your bunny should make more or less the same amount of soft and dry pellets every day. A large number of caecal droppings is often a sign that your pet is eating too much dried food, treats or alfalfa hay.

It is very important to find a good vet before your rabbit falls ill. Look for somebody who specialises in small animals – many vets are mainly interested in dogs and cats and are not very knowledgeable when it comes to rabbits. Other bunny owners may be able to point you in the right direction or your local rabbit club probably can help. Alternatively, look in the Yellow Pages and contact various surgeries in your area. Ask the nurse or vet if they see many rabbit patients. What is the price of vaccinations (myxomatosis and VHD)? How many rabbits has the vet neutered in the past year? Does the vet recommend spaying female rabbits? Don't hesitate to ask questions. If the vet seems offended or is not very helpful, you may want to go somewhere else.

Neutering

As your bunny reaches adulthood, it tends to be restless and more aggressive. Female rabbits become moody and both males and females may be less reliable with litter-training. An adolescent rabbit (particularly a buck) often sprays urine and performs the sexual act on people's arms, legs, slippers and other pets.

Neutering reduces or eliminates all these problems without changing your bunny's personality. If you own more than one rabbit, neutering can make it possible for them to live together happily, provided it is done early enough. Female bunnies should be spayed when they are six months old, male bunnies can be neutered earlier, when they are three to four months old. Neutering your doe is very important because nearly every female dies of uterine cancer when she is a few years old if she is not spayed. After being spayed, my rabbit stopped having false pregnancies and digging in the garden.

Illnesses

These are some of the most common illnesses and health problems rabbits may suffer from.

Bloat

If your bunny has a swollen, hard stomach and difficulty in breathing, it may have bloat. This is usually the result of eating too many greens, such as cabbage, lettuce, clover or wet grass. It can also be caused by spoiled food and mouldy hay, which should never be given to your bunny. Rabbits have a very sensitive bacterial flora in the intestine and the wrong food can cause certain kinds of organisms to multiply, resulting in excess gas production and a hard, distended tummy.

Bloat is a very serious condition and can be fatal, so take your bunny to the vet as soon as possible. In the meantime give your rabbit one or two teaspoons of caraway tea or half a teaspoon of liquid paraffin and gently massage its lower tummy to help break up the gas. Take away all bedding and food (including hay), but make sure your rabbit has plenty of fresh drinking water.

Constipation

If your bunny does not eat and makes very few droppings it may have constipation. Remove the dry food for a while and give your rabbit only hay and greens (for instance, endive, carrot and apple). Make sure your bunny has fresh drinking water and gets plenty of exercise.

You could also try giving a teaspoon of liquid paraffin, half a teaspoon of mineral oil or one to two teaspoons of caraway tea. If constipation continues for more than 24 hours take your bunny to the vet without delay.

Diarrhoea

Diarrhoea is not an illness in itself but a sign that something else is wrong. It can happen when the rabbit eats too many greens or wet grass or can be caused by stress, damp bedding, cold and draughts. It can also be the result of an infection or inflammation of the digestive system (see Coccidiosis). When a bunny has diarrhoea it makes very smelly and soft or runny droppings. It eats little or nothing and soon becomes weak and dehydrated.

Feed it only hay and perhaps a piece of dry brown bread or toast. Do not give any greens or foods high in protein (pellets, grains, alfalfa hay, etc) or any treats such as peanuts and sunflower seeds. The rabbit has lost a great deal of fluid so, as usual, be sure it has fresh drinking water. If necessary, wash the rabbit's bottom in mild soapy water and dry it thoroughly, then keep your pet warm. Disinfect the hutch and change the bedding and litter at least twice a day.

If your bunny does not get better within 24 hours, go to the vet straight away. You will need to take a stool sample for analysis.

Coccidiosis

Coccidiosis is a very serious illness which affects the intestine (intestinal coccidiosis) or the liver (hepatic coccidiosis). It is caused by microscopic parasites which live in the rabbit's intestine or liver and then are passed out with the faeces. These parasites reproduce very quickly (especially in moist areas) and can easily infect other rabbits.

Signs of coccidiosis include diarrhoea and a bloated tummy. The rabbit sits in a corner, shaking and grinding its teeth in pain. It becomes very thin and weak and may die unless something is done quickly.

If you think your bunny may be ill, take it to the vet immediately together with a stool sample for tests. Coccidiosis is highly contagious so clean the hutch and disinfect it thoroughly to prevent reinfestation.

Worms

If a bunny is eating normally but is not in good condition it probably has worms. These can sometimes be seen in droppings (but not always) and can be treated with a mild puppy wormer. Take a stool sample to the vet for analysis and ask advice on the best treatment.

Gastric hairballs

It is natural for a rabbit to swallow some fur during grooming. If your rabbit is moulting, or has long woolly hair, the ingested fur can gradually build up, blocking the passage of food from the stomach to the intestines. Bunny then eats less and less and its droppings are smaller and harder than usual.

You should give the sick bunny half a teaspoon of mineral oil or two teaspoonfuls of fresh pineapple juice (this contains an enzyme which helps break down the hairball). If the rabbit's condition does not improve, take it to the vet as soon as possible. Hairballs can be prevented by giving your pet regular exercise, feeding plenty of hay and brushing the coat frequently to remove the dead fur.

Sneezing

Sneezing and a runny nose may mean the rabbit has a cold. Give your pet plenty of hay and straw to keep it warm and sprinkle a few drops of oil of eucalyptus on the bedding. Sneezing can also be a reaction to bits of dirt in the air, dusty bedding or the use of strong disinfectants near your bunny.

Do not confuse occasional sneezing with a very serious respiratory illness called snuffles (see next page). Seek veterinary help if you're not sure.

Snuffles

Snuffles is a very serious condition which can lead to pneumonia (inflammation of the lungs) or even death. The symptoms are frequent coughing and sneezing, and a runny nose. The sick rabbit uses its front paws to wipe away the discharge, so the fur on the pads becomes wet and sticky.

If you think your bunny may be ill, take it to the vet immediately. Snuffles can be passed to other rabbits.

Fleas

Domestic bunnies sometimes catch fleas from cats and dogs, wild rabbits, poultry and other animals. When a bunny is infested, it scratches frequently and the skin becomes red and itchy. Fleas tend to gather mainly around the neck and the base of the ears. They sometimes act as carriers for other diseases, including myxomatosis, and can also bite humans.

Fleas multiply very quickly, laying their eggs just about anywhere: on the ground, in the carpet, bedding (human or pet), furniture and so on. A few days later the larvae emerge and the life cycle begins again.

It is very difficult to eliminate fleas once they have become established. You need to treat your house and garden as well as your rabbit, because if fleas are present in any of these places, they will continue to prosper.

There are various products you can use on your lawn or inside the house, and cleaning and hoovering frequently also helps to control infestation. Disinfect the hutch and run very thoroughly and wash your bunny with some medicated shampoo. Cat flea sprays and powders can be used but your bunny may become ill if it licks them during grooming. Repeat the treatment several times until you are sure that all the fleas are gone.

Ear mange or ear mites

If a bunny shakes its head and scratches behind its ears, it may have ear mites. These are microscopic parasites which burrow into the rabbit's skin causing itchiness and discomfort. Typical signs include loss of fur, red or flaky skin and brownish deposits inside the bunny's ears.

Put some olive or mineral oil on a ball of cotton wool and gently wipe inside the ears to soften the crusts. Alternatively, ask your vet to give you a lotion or cream to help clear up the mites.

It is important to clean the hutch thoroughly and change the bedding every day to prevent reinfestation. Avoid giving your bunny dusty hay or straw because this is where the mites may have come from in the first place. Ear mites are highly contagious and can be transmitted to other rabbits.

Fur mites

Bare patches in the fur, red flaky skin and brownish deposits may be a sign that your bunny has fur mites. Fur mites are very similar to the parasites causing ear mange and are usually found in the hair on the rabbit's shoulders and back. The skin itches, and the rabbit scratches itself frequently, making it easier for the infection to spread.

Bath the rabbit with a mild insecticide shampoo for puppies or kittens and take it to the

vet as soon as possible. Mites can be passed on to other pets as well as humans, so take care when you handle your rabbit. Do not forget to disinfect the hutch and accessories and change the bedding every day to avoid reinfestation.

Fly strike

Fly strike occurs when adult flies lay their eggs in faeces-soiled fur, usually under the rabbit's bottom. Within 12–24 hours the maggots emerge and start eating into the flesh, ultimately causing the rabbit's death. Fly strike is more common during the summer months so check your bunny twice a day for signs of infestation. If your pet does not keep its bottom clean, bath it regularly in mild soapy water, rinse and dry thoroughly. The best form of prevention is to spray your bunny with a suitable fly-killer (available from your vet). Keep the hutch clean and dry and change the bedding every day to prevent infestation.

Heat stroke

Your bunny is likely to get very hot in the summer if it does not have a shady corner in its hutch or enclosure. A rabbit with heat exhaustion lies down at full length and breathes very rapidly with its nostrils wide open. It gets very high temperature and may die if something is not done quickly.

Move the rabbit to a shady area straight away and apply a wet (not ice cold) flannel on its forehead, back and legs. Offer water at room temperature and feed half or one teaspoon of black coffee (depending on the size of your bunny) to improve circulation. Prevention is better than cure, so check that your rabbit's cage and run are set up in the right location (see pages 14–15).

Cuts and wounds
You can treat minor cuts and wounds using warm salted water (boiled and allowed to cool) or a mild antiseptic. Take your bunny to the vet straight away if the area becomes swollen and inflamed or if the eyes are affected. If your bunny is bleeding, apply some pressure to the wound and bandage it until a vet can see it.

Fractures
Fractured bones are usually the result of a rabbit being dropped or accidentally stepped on. A rabbit can injure its forelegs if it falls from a high place and lands badly, or it can break its spine if it kicks out suddenly with its back legs. It is very important to handle your pet properly to prevent accidents (see page 23). If you think your rabbit may have a broken limb, see the vet immediately. Broken forelegs can sometimes be repaired surgically but if the back is fractured the kindest thing to do is to put your bunny to sleep.

Overgrown teeth
A bunny's front teeth (incisors) continue to grow during its lifetime so it is important to give it something hard to nibble at to keep them in trim. A branch of willow or apple tree with the bark left on is ideal, or you can give your rabbit a block of untreated wood.

Sometimes a rabbit's lower jaw is longer than the upper jaw, so the two pairs of incisors cannot meet at the right angle. When this happens, the upper and lower front teeth do not wear each other down during chewing and they continue to grow. It could also happen that one of the incisors breaks off. The opposite tooth then does not have anything to grind against and keeps on growing, making it difficult for the bunny to eat normally.

Overgrown teeth should be trimmed by the vet or nurse every four to six weeks or you can learn to do this yourself. Clipping does not hurt your rabbit and takes only a few minutes.

Runny eyes
Dusty hay, draughts and specks of dirt can make your rabbit's eyes water occasionally. Wipe the eyes gently from the inner to the outer corner with cotton wool soaked in warm, salted water which has been boiled and left to cool. If the eyes are very red and swollen with a pus-like discharge in the corners, take your bunny to the vet straight away.

Sore hocks
Check the soles of your bunny's feet regularly to make sure there are no cuts or injuries. A rabbit may get sore hocks if the layer of fur under the feet is very thin, or if it is kept in a cage with a wire mesh floor. A small cut can become infected quickly and an abscess may develop.

Use an antiseptic ointment such as Preparation H and put your rabbit on a solid floor well padded with hay and straw. Changing the bedding every day will keep the rabbit's feet clean and dry and help the healing process. Do not clip the fur on the paws during grooming; if the hair is matted and dirty, simply bathe the feet in warm soapy water. If your bunny does not get better, take it to the vet as soon as possible.

Overgrown claws

Wild rabbits keep their toenails worn down naturally by burrowing. However, pet bunnies need to have their nails clipped from time to time, particularly if they live indoors and do not get much opportunity to dig or hop on hard surfaces.

To trim your bunny's claws, use a pair of special clippers available from most pet shops. Put the rabbit on a table or kitchen worktop and ask somebody to help you keep it still. In light-coloured rabbits it is easy to see the 'quick' or central part of the nail where the nerves and blood vessels are; but in dark-coloured animals this is virtually impossible. Hold your bunny's foot against the light or ask somebody to shine a torch under the nail to help you see the live part. The best method is to clip off only a little bit, cutting straight across the nail to avoid splintering.

Urine scald

Urine that remains for a long time on the delicate skin around the bottom and the inside of the back legs can cause severe irritation. To help relieve the discomfort, wash the rabbit in mild soapy water, rinse and dry thoroughly. If the skin is very sore, apply some Sudocream (available from the chemist) and take your bunny to the vet. Urine scald can be prevented by keeping the hutch clean and dry and changing the bedding and litter every day.

Myxomatosis

Myxomatosis is caused by a virus and can be transmitted by insect bite or through direct contact with an infected bunny. Within a few days the rabbit develops runny eyes and swellings on the face and genitals; these then break open, releasing a pus-like discharge which sticks to the bedding and food and brings on further infection. In the later stages, swellings appear all over the body, the rabbit goes off its food, has difficulty in breathing and gets very high temperature. The sick bunny usually dies after a few days. If it survives, it becomes resistant to the virus and cannot catch myxomatosis again.

There is no known treatment for myxomatosis, so avoid any contact between your pet and wild rabbits, which may be carriers of the disease without showing any of the signs. The best way of protecting your bunny is to have it vaccinated every 12 months.

Viral Haemorrhagic Disease (VHD)

VHD is a very serious disease which first appeared in Britain in 1992. It is caused by a virus and can be transmitted in a number of ways:

- through direct contact with another bunny;
- from water or greens contaminated by infected wild rabbits;
- wild mice, squirrels and rats carrying the virus;
- birds carrying the virus on their feet or in their droppings;
- people or other animals walking on contaminated (wild) rabbit droppings;
- blown on the wind or spread by insects such as flies;
- from somebody else's rabbit or another rabbit owner (people can carry the virus on their skin and clothes).

Baby rabbits under the age of eight weeks rarely catch VHD, but older rabbits usually die from the disease in just one or two days. They may look quite normal one day and suddenly die the next or they may become very ill before dying. They may have difficulty in breathing, lose their appetite and bleed from their nose and bottom. Occasionally a bunny gets only mildly ill and then recovers.

The best way of preventing your bunny from catching VHD is to have it vaccinated. Many vets now stock the vaccine or can order it for you and this will protect your pet for 6–12 months.

10 TRAVELLING

Even if your bunny is free to hop around the house and garden it is still likely to get bored after a while. To give your pet a change of scenery you could take it to the park, a field in the countryside or even on holiday with you.

Before you take your rabbit on an excursion, make sure that you are confident about handling and picking it up. It will help if the rabbit knows its name as well as the following commands: 'Come on/here' and 'It's OK' (see pages 25–26, 27). You will also need:

•a harness and a lead 3–5 metres (12–16ft) long. Practise putting the harness on your bunny well before your first outing so your pet has the chance to get used to it. Fasten the harness at home on a table or kitchen worktop, then all you have to do when you arrive is to clip on the lead.

•a travel cage in which your bunny can turn around and lie down comfortably. Always keep this handy — a predator is unlikely to harm your pet when it is in its cage.

It is a good idea to plan your trip in advance; ideally, you should be familiar with the place where you are taking your bunny. Check the weather forecast before you leave and allow plenty of time. Take a magazine, your (video) camera and maybe something to eat. Do not forget some water and food for your pet.

If you are travelling by car, drive as smoothly as possible so your bunny does not slide around in its cage and hurt itself. Do not smoke or play loud music. A vinyl transport cage can become very stuffy on a hot day so find a cool, shady spot to put it (not the boot of the car). If the journey is fairly long, stop every two hours and allow your bunny to stretch its legs in a safe and quiet spot. Do not forget to offer it water and something to eat.

When you arrive, let your bunny out of its cage as soon as it is safe to do this. Rabbits prefer to stay in the shade so look for a sheltered spot, preferably under a tree. Walking on hard surfaces such as a pavement or a road is important to keep your bunny's nails worn down, but on sunny days concrete can become very hot and you should be prepared to carry your bunny whenever necessary.

Your rabbit is bound to find the great outdoors intimidating at first. It will feel less worried if you sit next to it on the grass and try to reassure it. Soon your bunny will be busy looking around and marking its new territory and nibbling at various plants and weeds.

When you are out with your rabbit I strongly recommend that you use a harness and lead at all times; you will be able to retrieve your bunny and scoop it up quickly should danger arise. Having the rabbit on a lead means that your pet can never be too far from you but, even so, you should always keep a look out for traffic, animals and anything else which might frighten your companion.

If your rabbit is worried about something it will either hop back to you or run away and perhaps try to hide under a bush (expect the lead to get tangled from time to time). My advice is to keep the lead around your wrist rather than tied to a tree or a post: this way you will always know when your bunny is pulling at the lead, either because it is frightened or because it feels confident enough to move on.

It is not always easy to keep up with your bunny when it is on a lead. Rabbits do not walk in a straight line, but zig-zag all over the place, leaping and hopping back and forth. It is best to let your bunny take you where it wants to go rather than the other way round.

Above all, never pull or jerk roughly at the lead; react gently even in emergencies, when you should shorten the lead gradually and then quickly get hold of your rabbit. My tip is to use a retractible lead, which can be made longer or shorter depending on the situation.

Taking your bunny to the local park is not a good idea if:
- it is crowded: also, having a bunny will attract attention;
- it is noisy: children playing or loud traffic are bound to frighten your pet;
- the grass and plants have been sprayed with pesticides and other chemicals;
- dogs are roaming freely, as is often the case. Also, your bunny may fall ill if it grazes in a spot which is used by dogs to relieve themselves.

An open space in the countryside such as a meadow is a much better choice because:
- it is cleaner and quieter than a city park;
- it is easier to survey;
- if the area is not under cultivation it is less likely to have been treated with chemical weedkillers or insecticides;
- you probably will not find many dogs, but keep a look out for other animals which might harm your rabbit, including birds.

Finally, if you spend your holidays in this country, perhaps renting a cottage, why not take your bunny with you? You will probably have more time than usual to spend with your pet, which will be greatly appreciated, and your bunny will enjoy exploring unfamiliar surroundings and finding new ways of keeping busy.

Important note Make sure your bunny has been vaccinated against myxomatosis and VHD before you introduce it to the great outdoors. Always ask your vet for advice.

MY BUNNY

Name:_____

Date of birth:_____

Sex:_____

Breed:_____

Colour/description: _____

Weight:_____

Feeding guidelines:_____
_____

Favourite treats:_____

Favourite activity:_____

Likes:_____
_____

Dislikes:_____
_____

Vet's name: _____

Address: _____
_____

Phone number:_____

Surgery hours: _____

Medical notes:_____
_____

YOUR BUNNY'S PHOTO

Books

Lindsay, Anne, *Guide to owning a Rabbit,* TFH
Page, *Getting to know your Rabbit,* Interpet Publishing (for children)
Martin, Barry, *Rabbits as a new pet,* TFH
The official RSPCA pet guide, *Care for your Rabbit,* Harper Collins
Robinson, Howard, *Encyclopedia of Rabbits,* TFH

Magazines

Fur & Feather
Elder House
Chattisham
Ipswich
Suffolk IP8 3QE
tel: 01473 652 789
fax: 01473 652 788

Rabbits Only
PO Box 207
Hobrook
NY 11741
USA
tel: 001-516-737 0099
fax: 001-516-737 1905

Rabbits USA
PO Box 190
Colton
Oregon 97017
USA
tel: 001-503-824 2138

Useful addresses

When writing, please enclose a large s.a.e.
(stamped addressed envelope), or IRC
(International Reply Coupon).

British Rabbit Council
Purefoy House
7 Kirkgate
Newark
Nottingham NG24 1AD
tel: 01636 76042
fax: 01636 611683

The British Houserabbit Association
PO Box 346
Tyne & Wear NE99 1FA

National Rabbit Aid
108 Staple Hill Road
Fishponds
Bristol BS16 5AH
tel: 0117 956 3148
(to adopt a rescued bunny)

House Rabbit Society
1524 Benton Street
Alameda
CA 94501,
USA

INDEX